Mosaic Masterpieces in Needlework and Handicraft

Ann Roth

Mosaic Masterpieces in Needlework and Handicraft based on motifs from The Holy Land

Charles Scribner's Sons . New York

Copyright © 1975 Massada Press, Jerusalem

Photo Credits:
Pp. 8, 10, 12, 16, 18, 20, 22, 30, J. S. Schweig and the Israel
Exploration Society; 14, 26, Government Press Office;
24, National Parks Authority; 28, Israel Department of
Antiquities and Museums; color photographs, Chanan Sadeh

Designed by Zvi Narkiss

This book published simultaneously in the
United States of America and in Canada –
Copyright under the Berne Convention

PRINTED IN ISRAEL
Library of Congress Catalog Card Number 74-7799
ISBN 0-684-14062-4

CONTENTS

About 1,000 ancient mosaics, spanning a period of about 1400 years, have been uncovered in the Holy Land. The oldest of these mosaics date from the Hellenistic period (second century B.C.) and were discovered at Tell 'Anafa, in the Upper Galilee, near Kibbutz Shamir. The mosaics are of colored cubes set in geometric patterns. A chronological gap of approximately 100 years separates these with later mosaics.

The mosaic floors discovered at Massada, Herodion, Herod's winter palace at Jericho, as well as floors discovered in the Jewish Quarter of Jerusalem, date from the early Roman period (first century B.C.– first century A.D.). Part of these are in black-and-white inlay, which was typical of the style used during the reign of the Emperor Augustus. At Massada, and in the Jewish Quarter of Jerusalem, however, the mosaics were in rich and vivid color, and featured geometrical and floral patterns composed of labyrinths, meanders, vine leaves, olive leaves, rosettes, etc. The mosaics of the Synagogue at Ein Gedi, dating from the first half of the second century A.D., are a connecting link between this period and the Byzantine, which followed it. There are relatively few mosaics dating from this period compared to those found in later periods.

The art of mosaics began to flourish at the beginning of the fourth century, and reached its golden age in the Byzantine period, which lasted until 638 A.D. During this time, Byzantine emperors such as Constantine the Great, Theodosius II and his wife Eudocia, Zeno, Justinianus I, and Mauricius sponsored and encouraged the construction of vast numbers of buildings in the Holy Land. Churches, synagogues, public buildings, bathhouses, private homes, and burial chambers were among the wide variety of buildings constructed — and many of these were decorated with mosaic floors.

The end of the Byzantine period did not mark the end of mosaic art in the Holy Land. It continued to flourish without interruption through to the Crusader period (twelfth century A.D.). Some of the mosaic art that has come down to us from this period are the floors of the winter palaces of the Ummayyad caliphs (eighth century A.D.) at Khirbet el-Mafjar, near Jericho, and Khirbet el-Minya, near the Sea of Galilee, and the rich and impressive wall

An Introduction to Mosaic Art in the Holy Land

mosaics of the Dome of the Rock in Jerusalem (eighth century A.D.), and the twelfth-century wall mosaics from the Church of the Nativity in Bethlehem.

Limestone, which is soft, easy to cut, and found in abundance in the Holy Land, was the material most frequently used in the construction of the mosaics. The limestone was cut into small cubes, and set on a solid base of unhewn stones which had been covered with one layer of clay and another of fine cement. The pattern of the mosaic was drawn on the layer of cement before the cubes were set in. Polychrome floors generally consisted of three basic colors — white, black, and red. The richer the motif, the greater the number of colors added. When blues and greens were used, the cubes were generally of glass or marble, since these colors do not appear in limestone. Red cubes were sometimes of earthenware.

The sizes of cubes varied from floor to floor. The finer the quality of the floor, the smaller were the size of the cubes. The quality of mosaics are measured by the number of cubes used on a 4 x 4 inch surface. The cubes of monochrome floors are generally larger than those used in their polychrome counterparts, and number between 10 and 30 cubes per 4 x 4 inch area. Floors with simple decorations usually contain between 40 and 80 cubes per 4 x 4 inch area. Richly decorated floors generally contain between 90 and 120 cubes per 4 x 4 inch area. Where the design called for particularly delicate lines, for example, facial features, even smaller cubes were used. The Cock in the mosaic floor of the Church of the Nativity in Bethlehem contains between 450 and 500 cubes per 4 x 4 inch area. Stones were generally cut to a uniform dimension, but in cases where delicate features were to be represented, stones were cut to different sizes.

One of the fundamental problems that confronted the craftsman was orientation of the depiction in the floor. Was the head of his design to be closest to the door or furthest from it? This problem was compounded if the room had more than one door, or if the room had no pronounced direction. Another problem was the angle or view of the motif. The composition was intended for the person looking down at the design, which would not allow the viewer to see a large surface in uniform perspective.

Pattern books containing geometric, floral, and figurative designs were very often at the disposal of mosaicists in the Holy Land, and were handed down from generation to generation. These pattern books help to explain the similarity of designs found in synagogues and churches, as well as similarities in mosaics distant from each other both in time and in space. The local craftsmen were aided by the benefit of the experience and technical knowledge of craftsmen from other countries, but in a short time they managed to develop a local decorative style.

In an effort to solve these problems, craftsmen often decorated their floors with geometrical designs in which the symmetry was multilateral and the patterns repeated many times. Another common solution was the division of floors into small panels or medallions, which were then used for figurative motifs or inscriptions. This allowed craftsmen to adapt their designs to rooms of different shapes and dimensions. This technique also solved problems of proportion, since each panel was self-contained. A bird could be made the same size as a leopard in a bordering medallion. Examples of the medallion-technique are found in the mosaic floors of the Monastery of the Lady Mary, in a tomb in Beit Shean, at Beit Govrin, etc. Another solution was the placing of figures within a geometrical border, such as in the zodiacs at Beit Alpha, Huseifa, Khirbet Susiya, Na'aran, Hammat-Tiberias, and the Monastery of the Lady Mary.

Free compositions have been discovered in churches as well as synagogues. The floor of a church in Jerusalem contains a representation of Orpheus, surrounded by animals, playing his harp. The Church of the Miracle of the Multiplication at et Tabgha contains free-form Nilotic scenes. Several synagogue floors contain free-form representations of biblical scenes such as the Sacrifice of Isaac (Beit Alpha), Noah's Ark (Gerasa), Daniel in the Lion's Den (Na'aran), and Orpheus-David (Gaza). Because craftsmen chose to solve problems of composition by the use of medallions or panels, very few examples of free composition exist.

Since mosaics served to decorate buildings dedicated to widely different purposes, they are of vastly different qualities, and range from delicate and perfect design of human figures to rough designs which are simple craftwork.

Asher Ovadiah
Department of Classical Studies and Art History
Tel Aviv University.

Birds on Lotus Flowers

CHURCH OF THE MIRACLE OF THE MULTIPLICATION
OF THE LOAVES AND FISHES, ET TABGHA

The Church of the Miracle of the Multiplication of the Loaves and the Fishes (middle fifth century) is located at et Tabgha, on the northwestern shores of the Sea of Galilee. It is here, according to tradition, that Jesus fed a multitude with only five loaves of bread and two fishes. The church contains three mosaics. The smallest, positioned behind the altar, depicts the symbols of the miracle: a basket of bread marked with crosses, and a fish at either side. Two other mosaics, each a rectangular panel brimming with Nilotic birds and wild flowers and bordered by lotus flowers, flank the BEMA.

BIRDS ON LOTUS FLOWERS
(DETAIL, TRANSEPT PAVEMENT).
A graceful array of storks, herons, flamingoes, and other birds nest and feed among bullrushes, thistle, and oleander bushes. The scene is reminiscent of wildlife of the Nile area.

Ark of the Law

BEIT ALPHA SYNAGOGUE, BEIT SHEAN VALLEY

The Beit Alpha Synagogue (early sixth century) was accidentally uncovered by kibbutz members digging an irrigation channel in 1928. The mosaic floor, consisting of three panels — the Ark of the Law, the Zodiac, and the Sacrifice of Isaac (not shown here) — is remarkably well preserved and perhaps the most childlike, provincial, and disproportionate of all mosaics found in the Holy Land — and therein lies its charm.

ARK OF THE LAW. The ritual motif depicted here was probably designed to duplicate the actual contents of the apse. The Ark of the Law, an eternal light suspended from its gabled roof, is seen through a parted ritual curtain. Birds and seven-branched candelabra flank the Ark, along with rams' horns, palm branches, citrons, and incense shovels. The Ark is guarded on either side by a lion.

Zodiac

BEIT ALPHA SYNAGOGUE, BEIT SHEAN VALLEY

ZODIAC. *Although astrology was always considered alien to the Jewish religion, this motif formed the central panel of the synagogue floor. The panel is composed of two concentric circles set within a square. The outer circle contains the twelve signs of the zodiac, with their Hebrew names. Counterclockwise, they are:* SARTAN *(Cancer, crab);* ARYEH *(Leo, lion);* BETULAH *(Virgo, virgin);* MOZNAYIM *(Libra, scales);* AQRAB *(Scorpio, scorpion);* KASHAT *(Sagittarius, archer);* GEDI *(Capricorn, goat);* DELI *(Aquarius, water bearer);* DAGIM *(Pisces, fishes);* TALEH *(Aries, ram);* SHOR *(Taurus, bull);* TEOMIM *(Gemini, twins). The inner circle shows the sun-god, Helios, driving a chariot drawn by four galloping horses through a moon- and star-studded sky. At each of the four corners is the personification of a season, represented by the winged and jewelled bust of a woman, surrounded by seasonal fruits and birds. Counterclockwise from the upper left, they are:* TEKUFAT NISAN *(spring);* TEKUFAT TAMUZ *(summer);* TEKUFAT TISHRI *(autumn);* TEKUFAT TEVET *(winter).*

Duck

APODYTERIUM, TIBERIAS

Bathhouses, introduced to the Holy Land by the Romans, were very popular in the Byzantine period. The Tiberias climate, as well as its location on the shores of the Sea of Galilee made it ideal for baths. The floor of the bathhouse (late sixth century) is composed of a series of interlaced ovals and irregularly shaped medallions set within a decorative frame. As a protective measure, the floor was recovered with earth shortly after it was excavated.

DUCK (DETAIL). *Birds and fish are the subject of this highly vivid and naturalistic mosaic which formed part of the floor of the Apodyterium, or dressing room, which adjoined the Roman-style bath.*

Tree with Gazelles

HISHAM'S PALACE, KHIRBET EL-MAFJAR

Hisham's Palace (first half eighth century) contains the only known instance of the use of figurative representation in Arabic art. The palace was built by Hisham ibn Abd el Malik for use as the winter residence of the caliphs of the Ummaiyyad dynasty. The mosaic floors of the palace are paved in geometric, carpet-like designs which are a marvel of exactness.

TREE WITH GAZELLES.
Simple in conception, this mosaic depicts two gazelles peacefully grazing in the shade of an exquisite fruit tree, undisturbed as a third falls prey to a hungry lion. The Hellenistic Oriental tradition is expressed both in the subject and in the form of the animals.

Black Man Leading Animal

The Monastery of the Lady Mary (second half sixth century) contains five rooms, each of which is paved with a mosaic. The smallest of the rooms contains a mosaic with a grape-harvest motif. A vine-tendril, emerging from an amphora, creates a pattern of interconnected medallions, enclosing a wide variety of naturalistic scenes. The twelve medallions include the harvest, a man playing with a dog, a man leading a donkey, and a black man leading an animal. Filling in the spaces between the medallions are birds, animals, and clusters of grapes.

BLACK MAN LEADING ANIMAL (DETAIL). *Simple and naive in design, this disproportionate scene shows a man leading what might be a giraffe, but what could also be a camel.*

Seven-Branched Menorah

MAON SYNAGOGUE, NIRIM

The mosaic floor of the Maon Synagogue (first half sixth century) is framed by a decorative border of stylized flowers set between rows of triangles. The field is composed of fifty-five medallions, interconnected by vine-tendrils, leaves, and clusters of grapes. Animals, plants, and Jewish ritual objects occupy the medallions in this highly symmetrical composition. There are humorous touches in the design, such as the medallion depicting a chicken laying an egg.

SEVEN-BRANCHED MENORAH (DETAIL). *Of all Jewish ritual objects, the seven-branched candelabrum is the oldest and probably best-known. Here it occupies a central position, in the space of two medallions, and is flanked by rams' horns and clusters of grapes. The legs of the menorah are in the shape of lions' paws.*

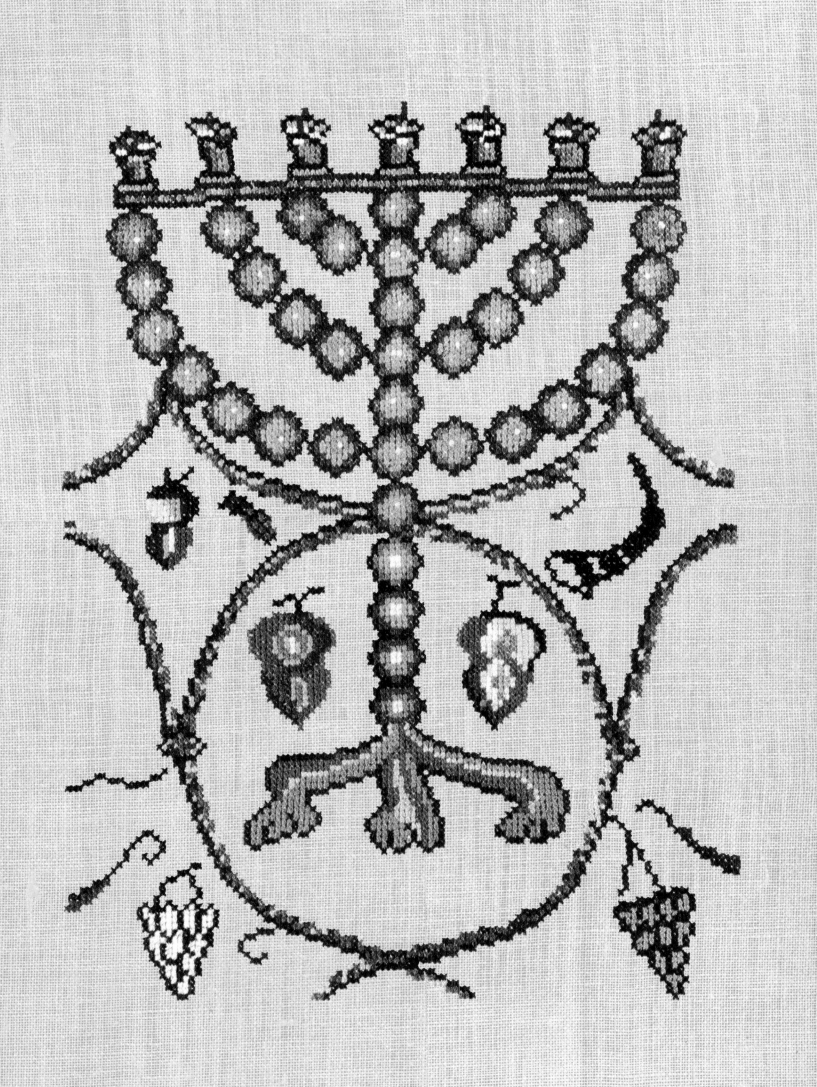

Leopard

MAON SYNAGOGUE, NIRIM

LEOPARD (DETAIL). *Representation of animals and birds of all kinds was a favorite subject of Byzantine mosaicists. The leopard shown here is not native to the Holy Land and it is likely that the design was taken from artists' copybooks which were in general circulation.*

Pelican

CHURCH OF CAESAREA

The coastal city of Caesarea, the seat of Roman governors and capital of the Holy Land for over 500 years, and later rebuilt as a Crusader city, is today a treasure-house of archeological riches. Among the remaining structures are: a church floor (late sixth century), uncovered on a small hill out-side the city walls; a Roman aqueduct and Hippodrome; a synagogue which dates to the second-fourth centuries A.D.; and a twelfth-century Crusader wall surrounding the city.

PELICAN (DETAIL, ATRIUM PAVEMENT). *Interlaced medallions form the pattern for this highly naturalistic mosaic. Represented are pheasants, peacocks, storks, leopards, foxes, lions, wild boar, elephants, deer, and pelicans.*

Geometric Patterns

CHURCH OF SHAVEI ZION, NORTH OF ACRE

The Church of Shavei Zion (early fifth century) was uncovered in 1955. The nave, the narthex, and the aisles were decorated with mosaic pavements of simple geometric designs.

GEOMETRIC PATTERNS (DETAIL, NAVE). *This geometrical design is typical of the period when the church was attempting to develop a symbolism of its own. The design in the upper and lower left hand corners, consisting of two overlaced links, is known as Solomon's Knot and was a common design of the period.*

Decorative Borders

BEIT SHEAN, MONASTERY OF THE LADY MARY;
CHURCH OF SHAVEI ZION

Almost all mosaics consist of a field framed within a border. Borders may be of the simple kind, using just one recurring geometric theme. At other times, highly sophisticated composite or multiple decorative borders are used. Among the patterns frequently found are the braid, the double braid, the single straight line, and fringe.

DECORATIVE BORDERS. The borders shown here were taken from the mosaic pavements of the Monastery of the Lady Mary in Beit Shean. They frame a detail from the aisle of the Church of Shavei Zion. This floor was adorned with a central jewelled medallion with a cross and three chevrons, two stylized fish, and pomegranates.

Decorative Borders

BEIT SHEAN, MONASTERY OF THE LADY MARY;
KHIRBET EL-MINYA

Khirbet el-Minya (eighth century) was built in the Ummaiyyad period and probably served as the fortified castle of a rich landowner. It stands in a very fertile area on the northwestern coast of the Sea of Galilee. It was an important station in the caravan road from Egypt to Syria. Mosaic floors of geometric designs were uncovered in several rooms.

DECORATIVE BORDERS. The intertwined braid shown here is a detail from a mosaic pavement of Khirbet el-Minya. The lower border is from one of the rooms of the Monastery of Lady Mary in Beit Shean.

Interior with Samples

1 TEA-COSY, made from the same materials used in the model on page 17. The tree motif was embroidered twice, and then joined to a strip embroidered with cable borders. The colors of the cable are the same as those in the tree. Patterns for design and border appear on pages 48–49, and 60–61.

2 CUSHION, a color variation of the cable motif on page 31. Sudan wool and sudan canvas were used.

3, 4 CUSHION AND TABLECLOTH, both made from even-weave fabric with 18 threads per square inch using whole threads of DMC embroidery silk. The chain motif is here used as a closed border. In order for colors to show the correct follow-up, the number of chains, including corners, should be divisible by three.

5 RUG, using the design on the lower part of the Ark (page 11). The motif is repeated twice; the border at the bottom of the design was incorporated both at the bottom and top of the rug. Smyrna wool and smyrna canvas were used.

6, 7 WALL HANGING AND MOSAIC TILE, based on design on page 27. Sudan wool and sudan canvas were used for the wall hanging. Small square stones were glued to a white board for the mosaic effect.

8 BELT, made from evenweave fabric with 18 threads per square inch. The design here is the same as the one used in cushion and tablecloth (3, 4).

General Instructions

The color plates on pages 9–31 show the embroideries in their original sizes. The needlework is mainly cross-stitch and only occasionally is straight-stitch used to accentuate the outlines. Fine evenweave fabric with 30 threads per inch was used for the models.
The designs on pages 9, 11, 15, 19, 23, 25, 29 and 31 show a background partly filled in with cross-stitch.
For the motifs on pages 23 and 31 DMC 677 was used; on page 15, DMC 842; and on page 29, off-white; the other motifs were filled in with DMC 739.
The cross-stitches are worked in oblique lines.
In this way the different elements of the design are linked together, avoiding too massive a result.

Color indications for each design are given according to the color-chart of DMC embroidery silk. On this fine fabric 2 strands of silk were used.

The samples on pages 32 and 33 show the use of these designs in varying techniques. In all these cases the patterns given in this book can be used. An exception must be made for the design on page 13. The straight-stitch is used here very frequently. This can only be done in combination with the cross-stitch. Omitting the straight-stitch will alter the color setting too much.

If worked with other materials the colors will differ more or less from the originals. The color-chart on the back flap can be useful in finding the right colors.

The motifs on pages 27, 29 and 31 can be repeated as often as necessary, and all color variations are possible. Examples are given on pages 36 and 38. The chain-border needs three times three colors, each chain containing three shades, combined with a bright color on a dark background, or a dark color on a bright background. Both right and left corners can be found on the patterns, making it possible to embroider closed borders.

The use of different materials will be discussed under techniques.

Color Chart

These numbers refer to DMC embroidery silk.

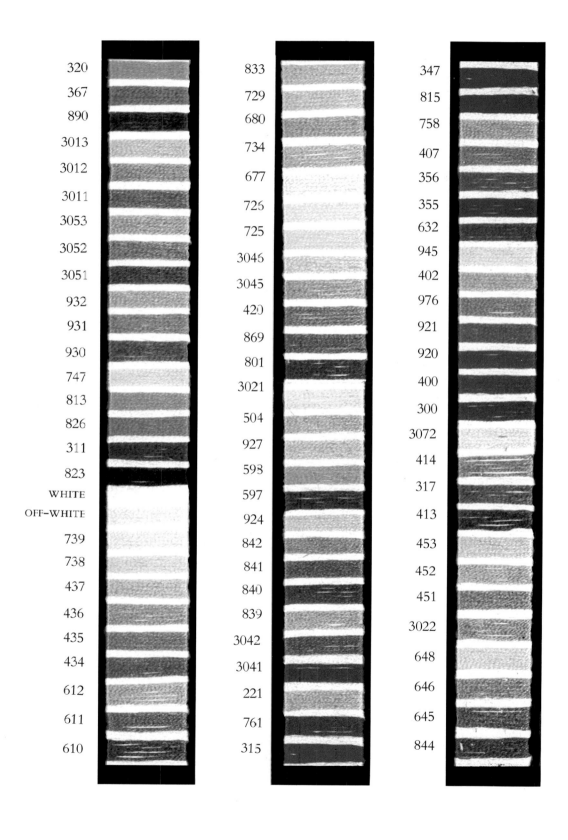

320	833	347
367	729	815
890	680	758
3013	734	407
3012	677	356
3011	726	355
3053	725	632
3052	3046	945
3051	3045	402
932	420	976
931	869	921
930	801	920
747	3021	400
813	504	300
826	927	3072
311	593	414
823	597	317
WHITE	924	413
OFF-WHITE	842	453
739	841	452
738	840	451
437	839	3022
436	3042	648
435	3041	646
434	221	645
612	761	844
611	315	
610		

Smyrna Technique

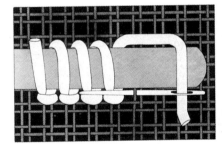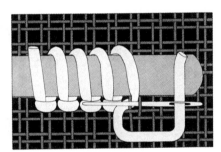

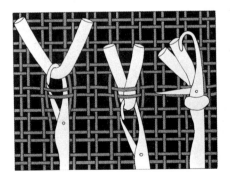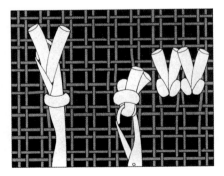

Since the motifs in this book were originally floor designs, they are all suitable to be put on floors again. The smyrna technique is most suitable for this purpose.

Smyrna-wool and smyrna-canvas are the best materials for making rugs and carpets. Sudan materials are more advisable for smaller objects since dimensions would become too large if smyrna materials were used.

Two methods can be followed in the smyrna technique. The first method uses a needle and a small lath. A long thread is worked around the lath, row by row. The nooses of several rows are cut together. The second method uses cut threads. The length of the threads depends on the desired pile and on the thickness of the wool. To cut the wool, special laths are available in needlework shops. Cutting can be done easily, using a Stanley knife. A so-called smyrna-needle (a special crochet needle) is used to make the knots, one by one, as shown in the illustration.

For the patterns in this book, since many colors have been used, the second method is best. Each square of the pattern represents one knot. The background must always be filled in with a neutral color. The sides can be given a finishing touch by making a braid-border. The canvas is folded back two holes outside the knotting work. A long woollen thread the color of the outside border is used to make long stitches around the canvas, taking four holes to the right, three holes to the left, working back and forth. The needle is always placed at the backside of the canvas. At the corners several stitches are made in the same hole, to cover the canvas completely. This border is very beautiful for cushions as well as rugs. The size, if smyrna wool and smyrna canvas are used, will be four times the size of the original; if sudan materials are used the size will be three and one half times that of the original.

Kelim Technique

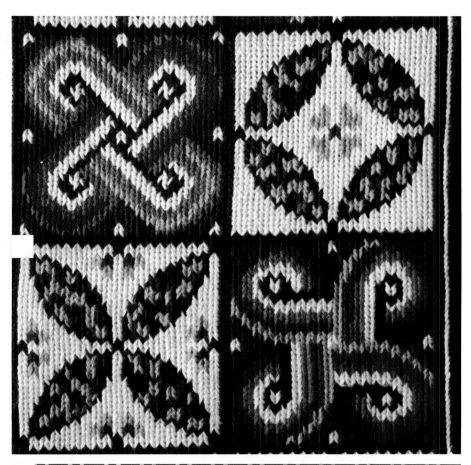

This technique is suitable for cushions, runners, and small rugs. Sudan wool and sudan canvas suit this technique best although small objects such as cushions can be made with tapestry wool and tapestry canvas.

The stitch has a V-form, like a mesh-stitch. The work must be done in rows, working half the V from top to bottom, the other half next to it from bottom to top. Each square in the pattern represents half the V. In the vertical direction the stitches pass two threads of the canvas, as shown in the illustration. It is preferable to work either with more than one color at the same time, or to do the outlines first, to avoid errors in working in the right direction. The background must always be filled in with a neutral color. The size, if worked with the sudan material, will be three and one half times the size of the original; if tapestry wool and tapestry canvas are used the size will be one and one half times that of the original.

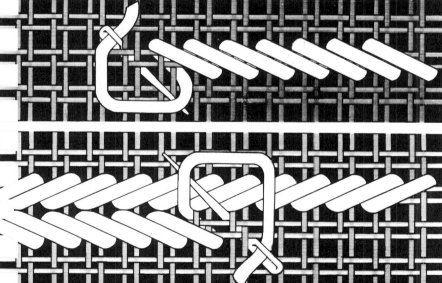

Cross-Stitch Technique

Cross-stitch is one of the oldest and most popular techniques. The choice of the material is very important. Every even-weave fabric which has the same number of threads per inch in each direction of the fabric is suitable. The use of DMC embroidery silk is preferable, as the number of used strands can be adapted to the coarseness of the fabric. Moreover, this material has the greatest number of colors available.

The best results are obtained if worked as much as possible from bottom up, thus forming a half cross up to the end of the row, completing the other half as shown. Start, as a rule, at the center of the pattern, marking the center of the fabric with a thread. It is also preferable to start with the darkest colors. The use of straight-stitches is mentioned on the pattern. The used lines are to be found in the color indications. Straight-stitches must always be made after finishing the cross-stitches.

To avoid confusing the shades it may be helpful to glue a thread of the appropriate color beside each number.

Apart from the already-mentioned materials, tapestry wool and canvas can be used. In this case only half crosses are made on the canvas. This technique is very suitable for cushions, chairs, etc. The background must always be filled in with a suitable neutral color. The size will be one and one half times that of the original.

Mosaic Technique

The sample in this book was made with Talens mosaic stones, measuring 2/5 square inch. Since few colors are available, the result will differ considerably from the originals. Nevertheless, starting with the basic colors red, green, blue, etc., good results can be obtained. A mixture of bright colors will make the background look more natural.

The stones must be glued row by row according to the pattern. Use a good hobby adhesive. The underlayer can be cardboard, glass, or wood. If a nice underlayer is used, glueing just the motif will be sufficient; on other materials the background must be filled in with neutral bright colors. The size will be six times that of the original.

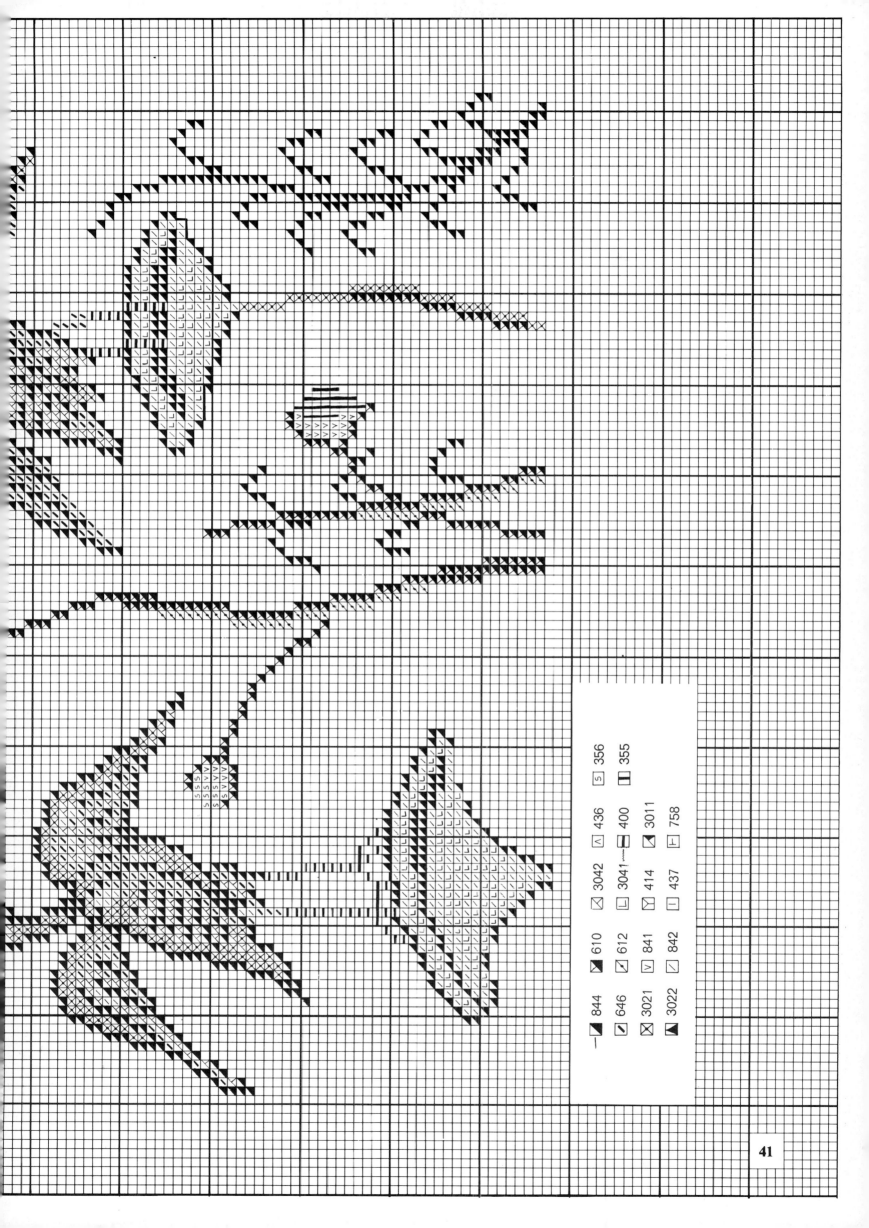

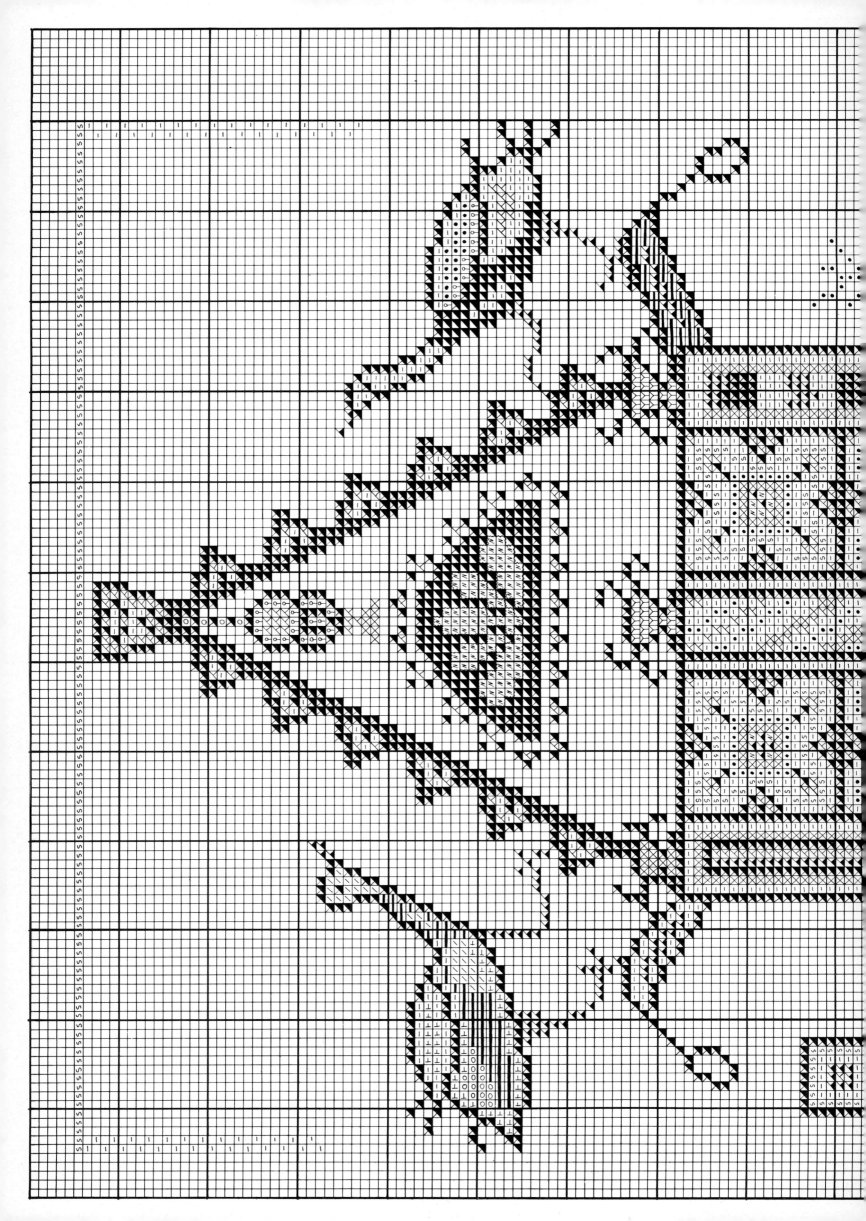

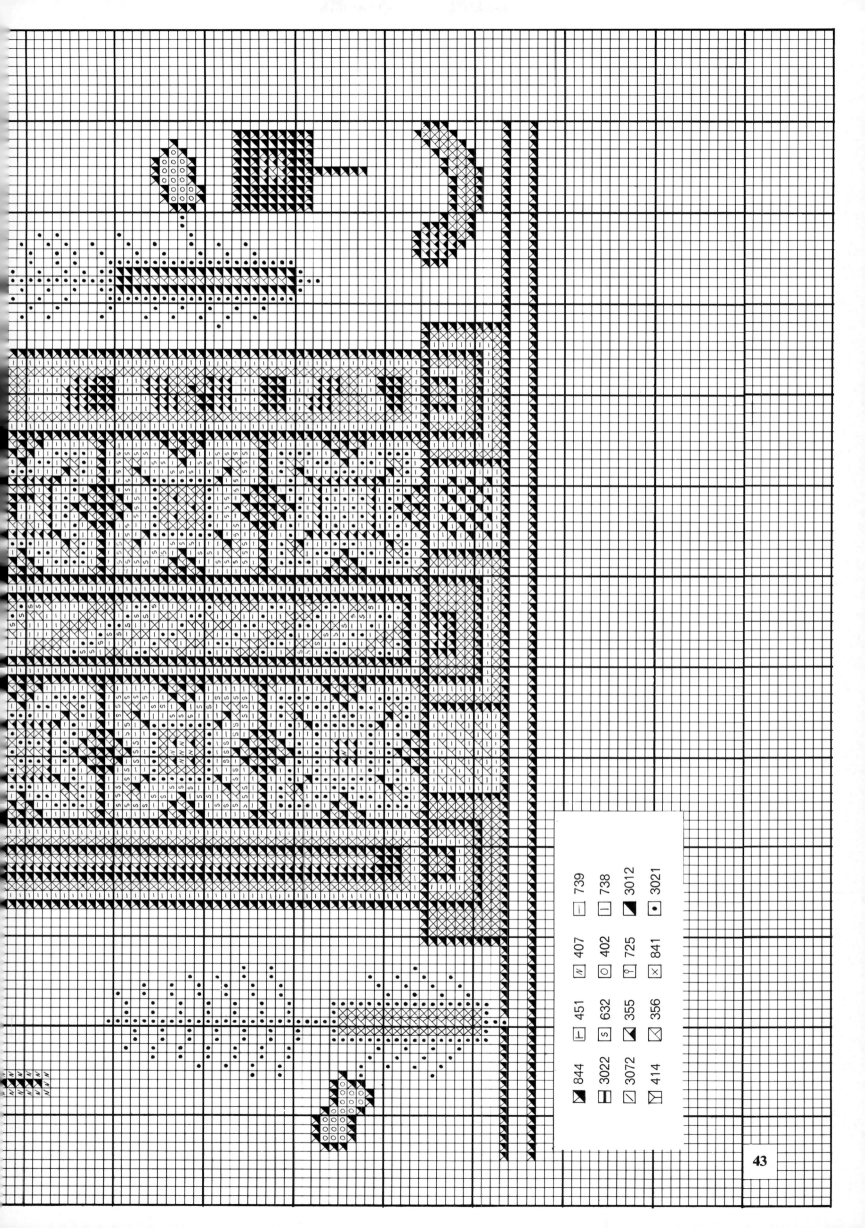

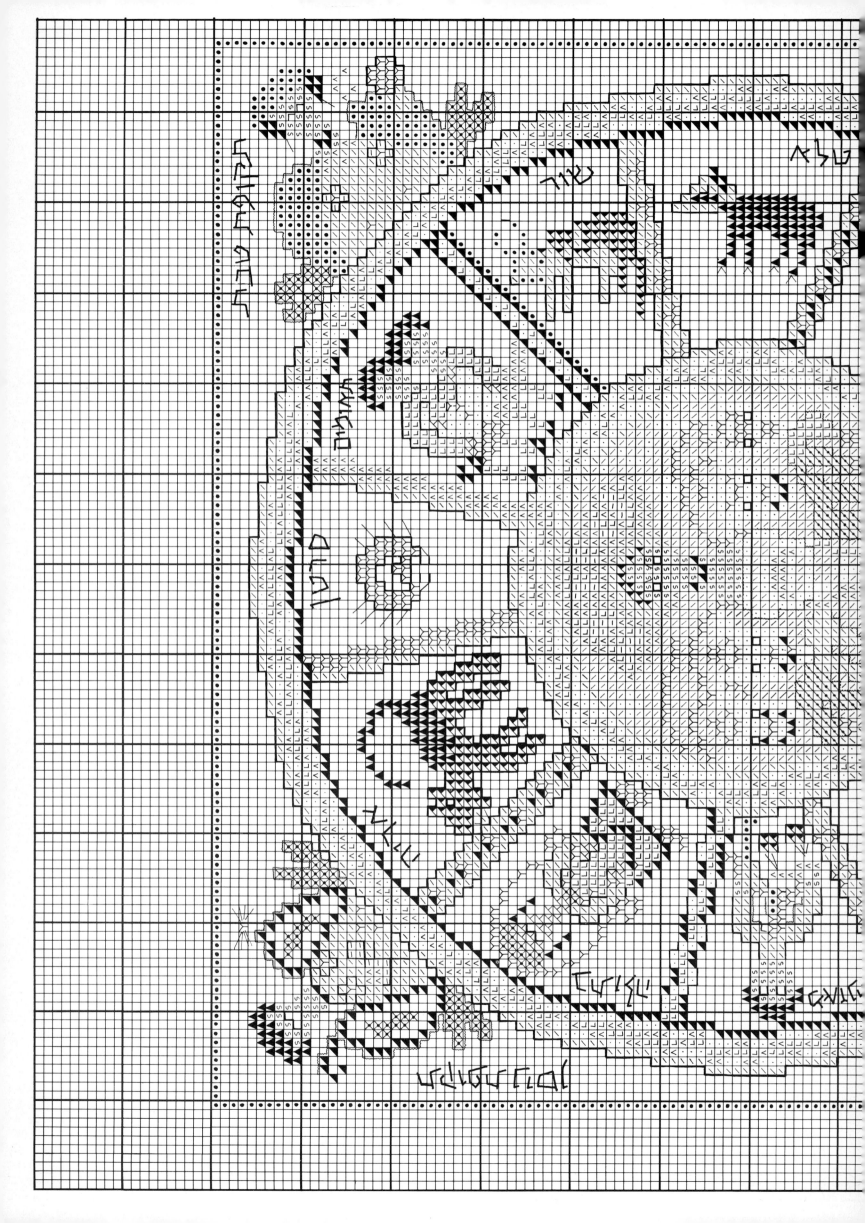

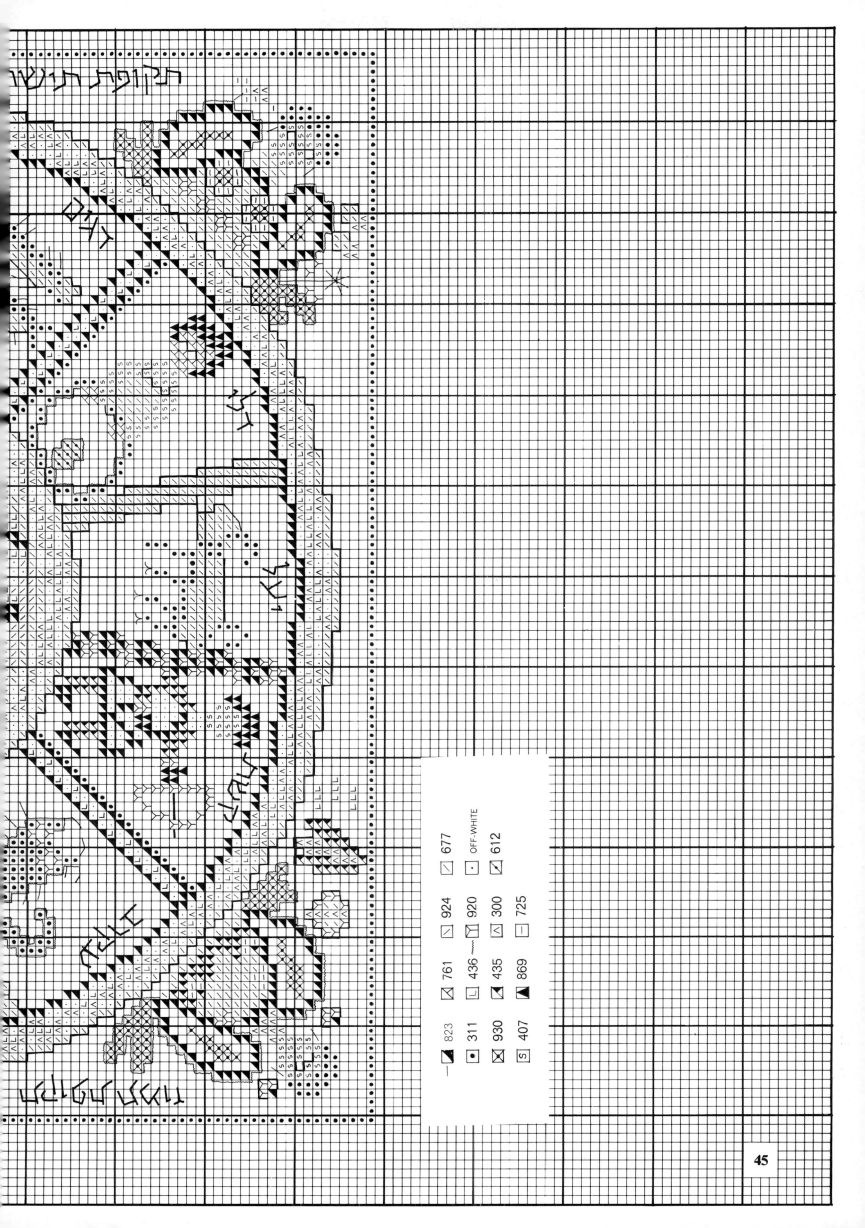

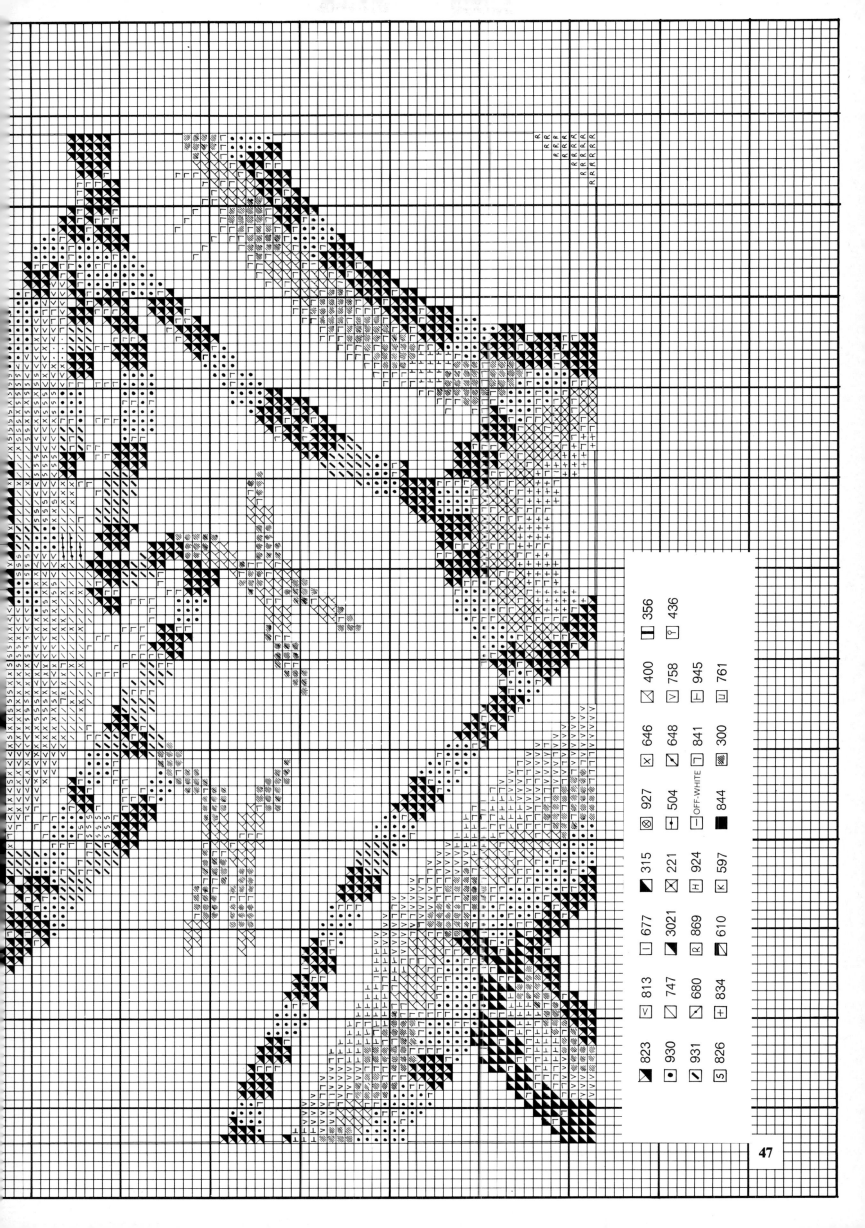

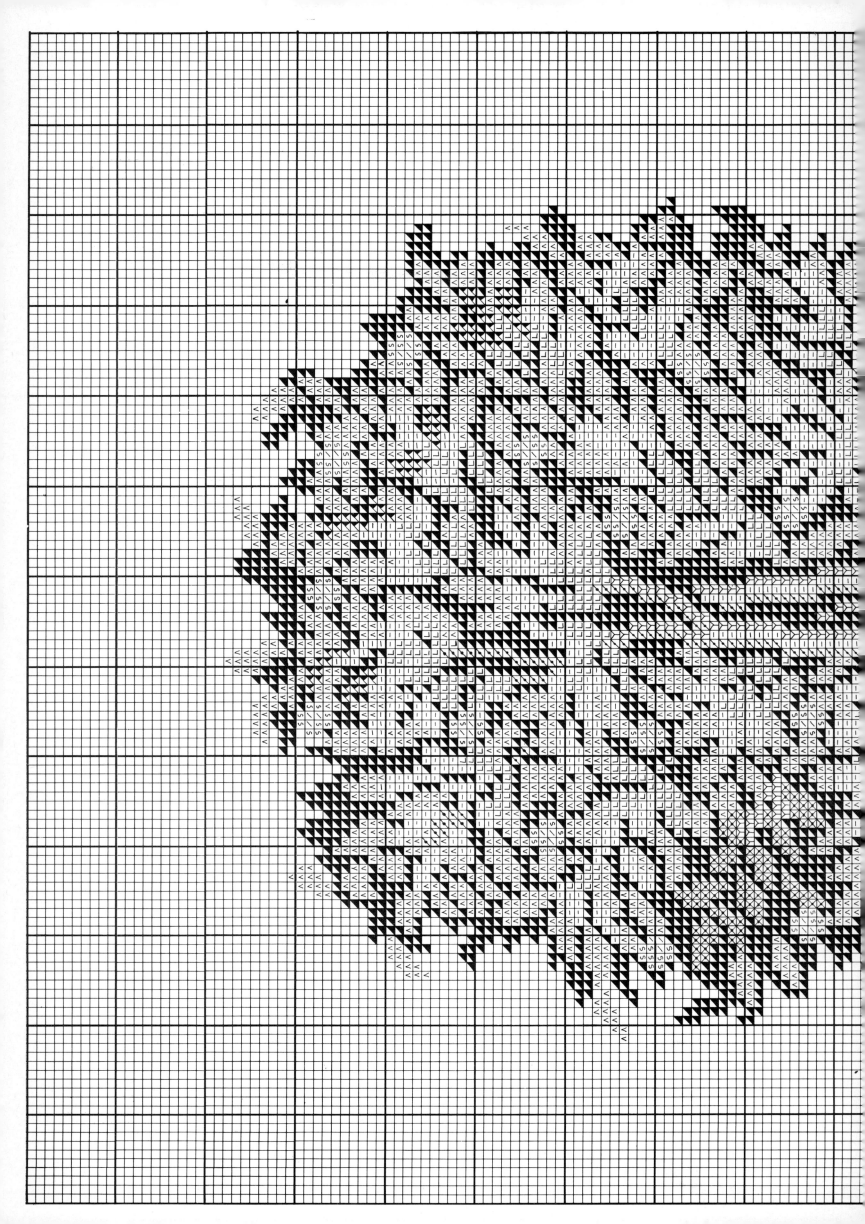

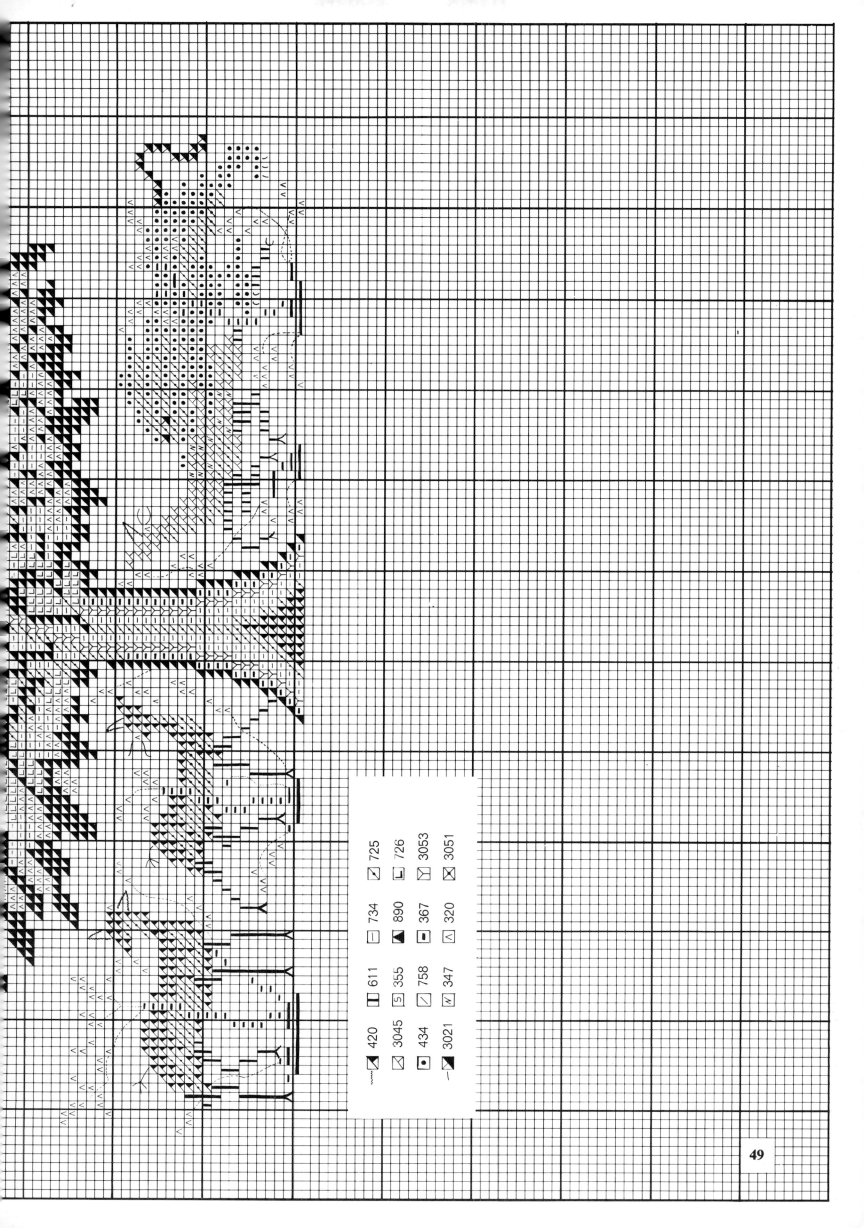

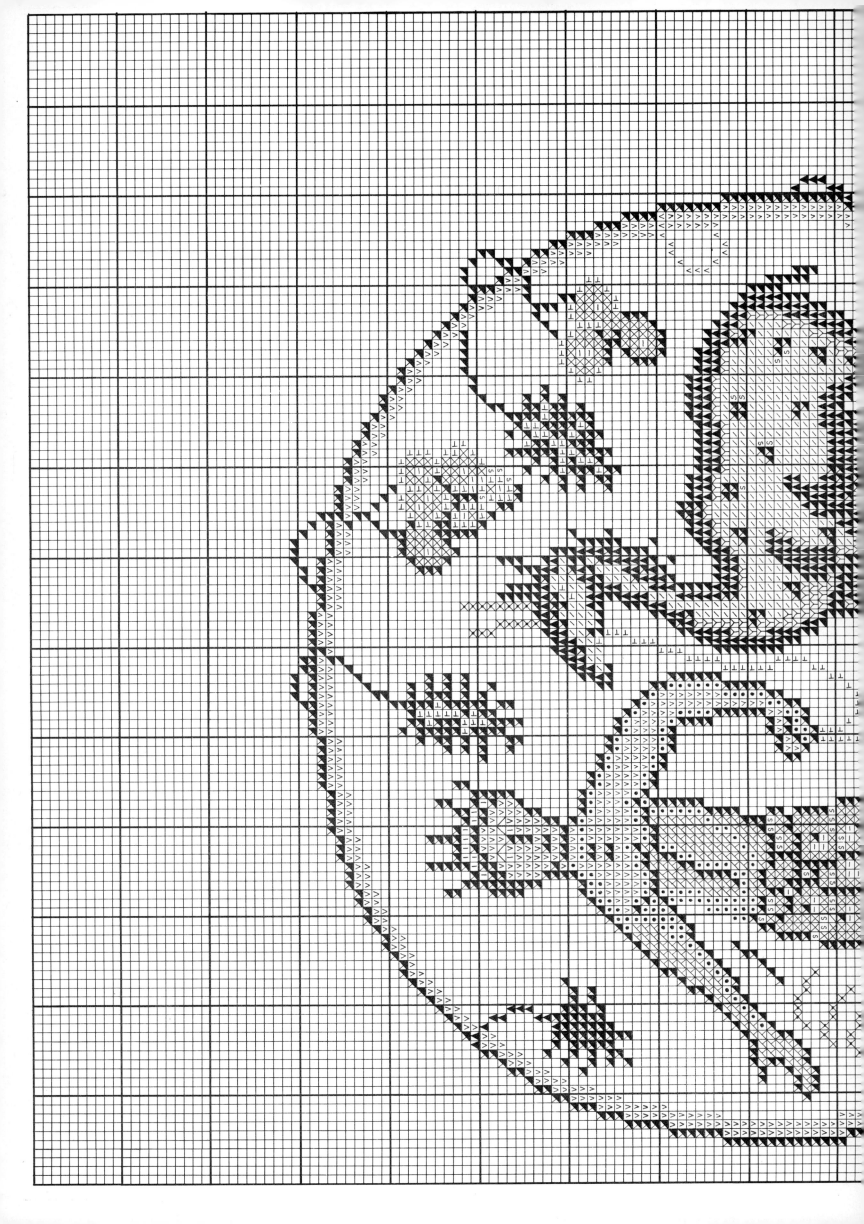

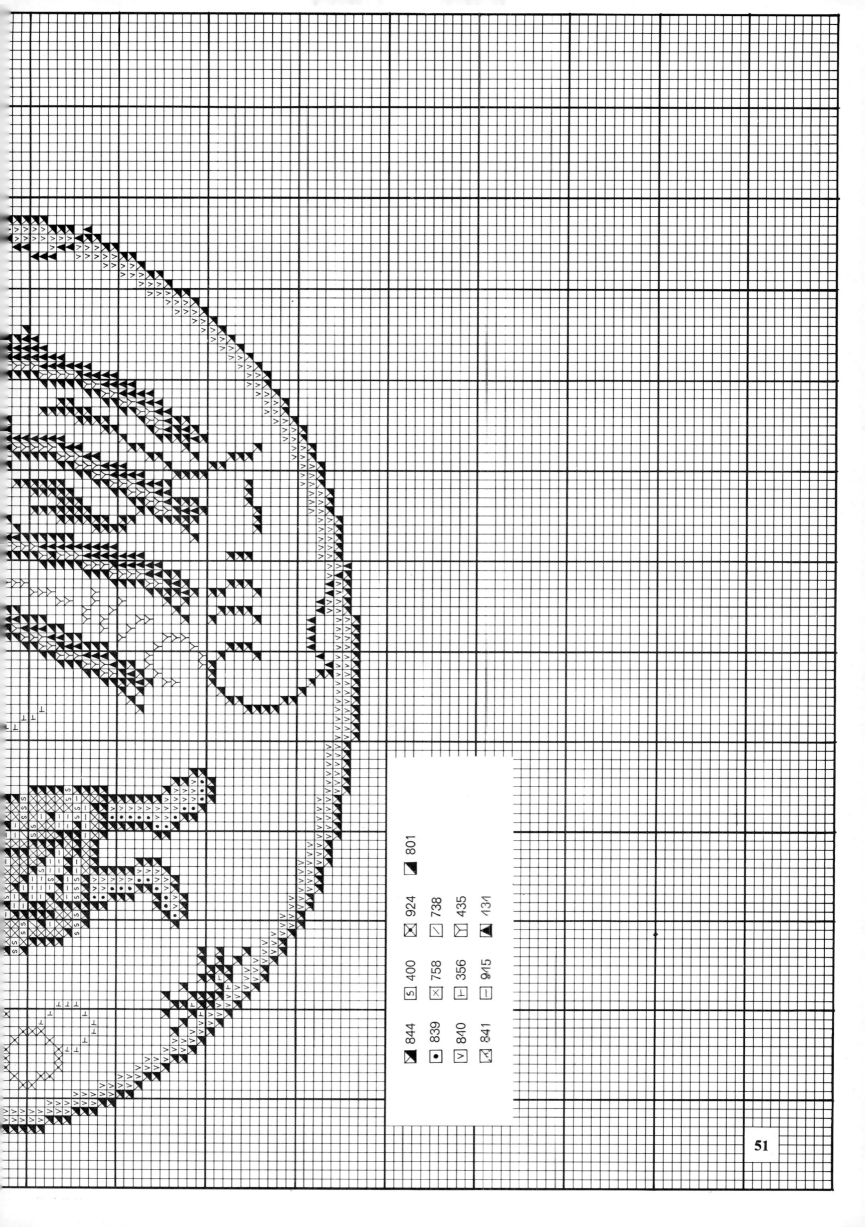

◨ 844	⑤ 400	⊠ 924	◣ 801
• 839	⊠ 758	╱ 738	
∨ 840	⊢ 356	⅄ 435	
⊠ 841	⊡ 915	◢ 131	

51

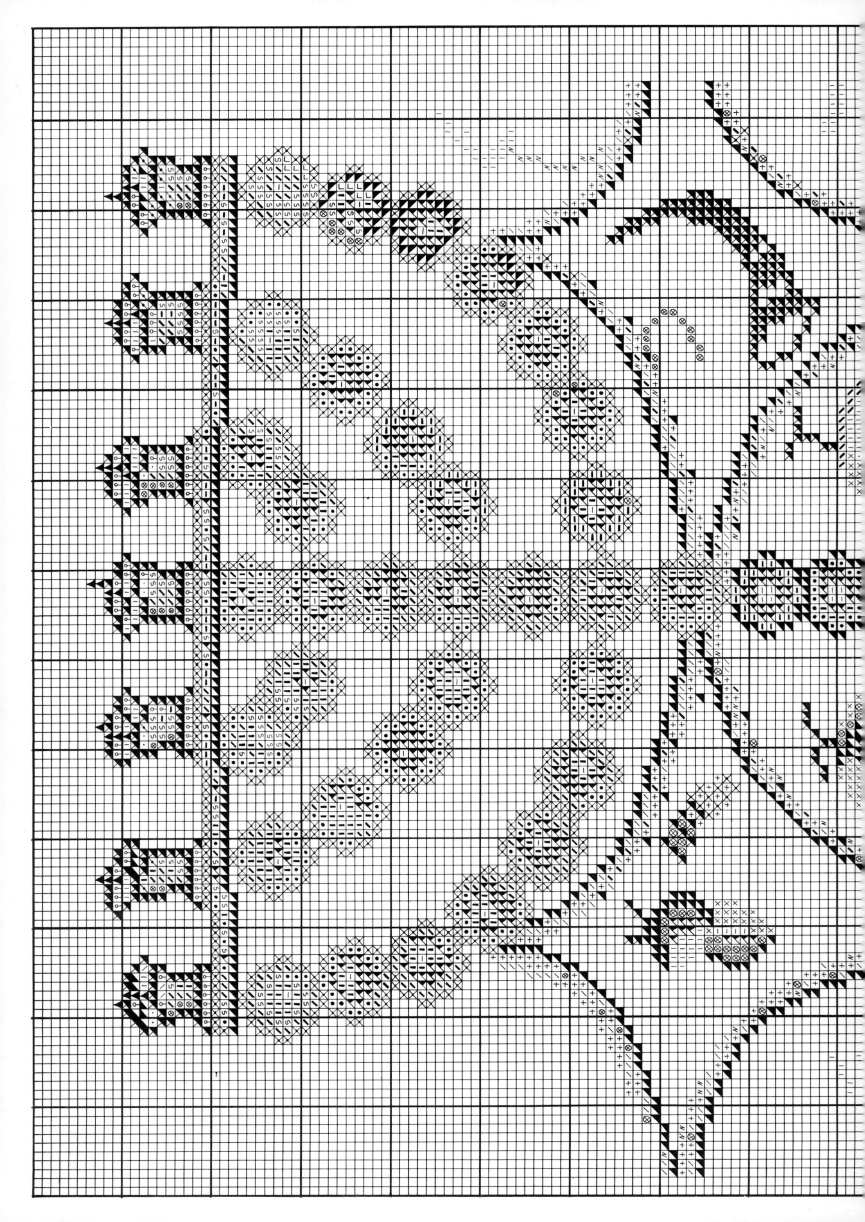

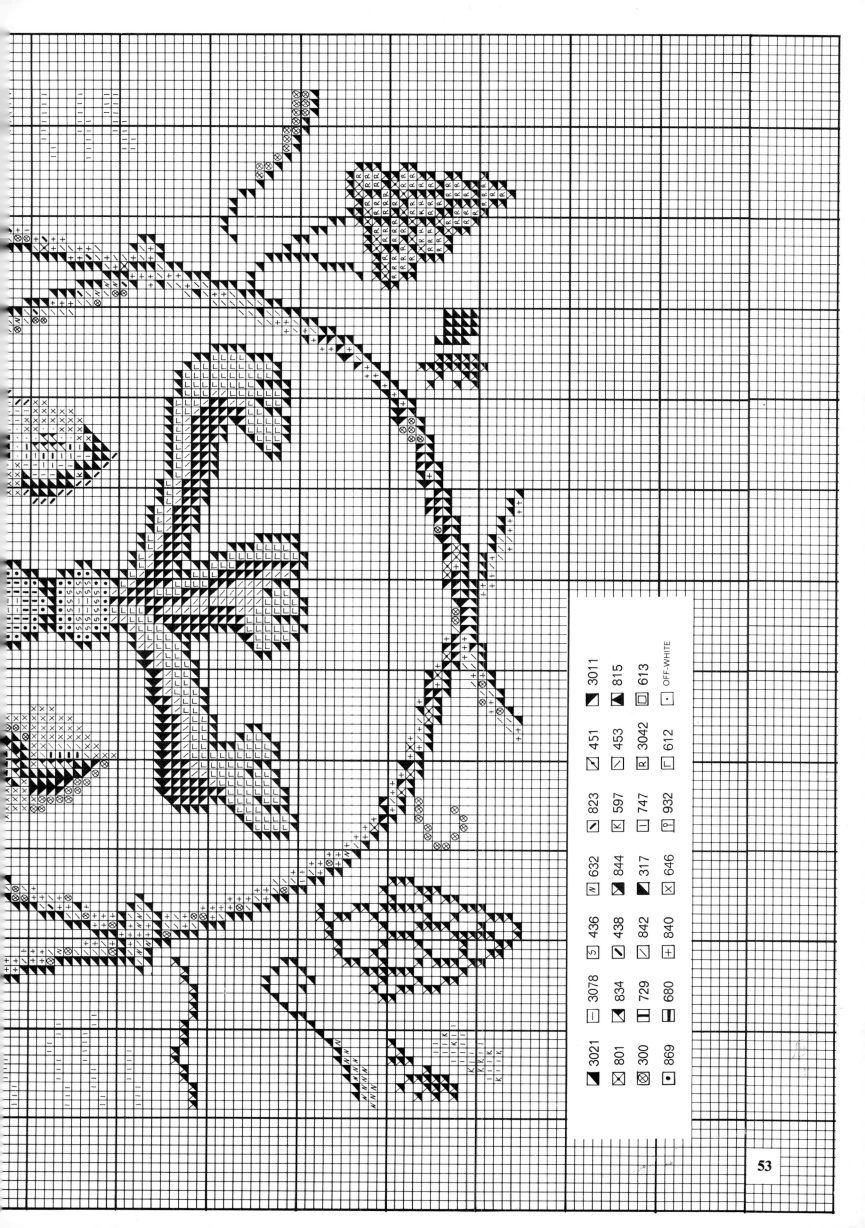

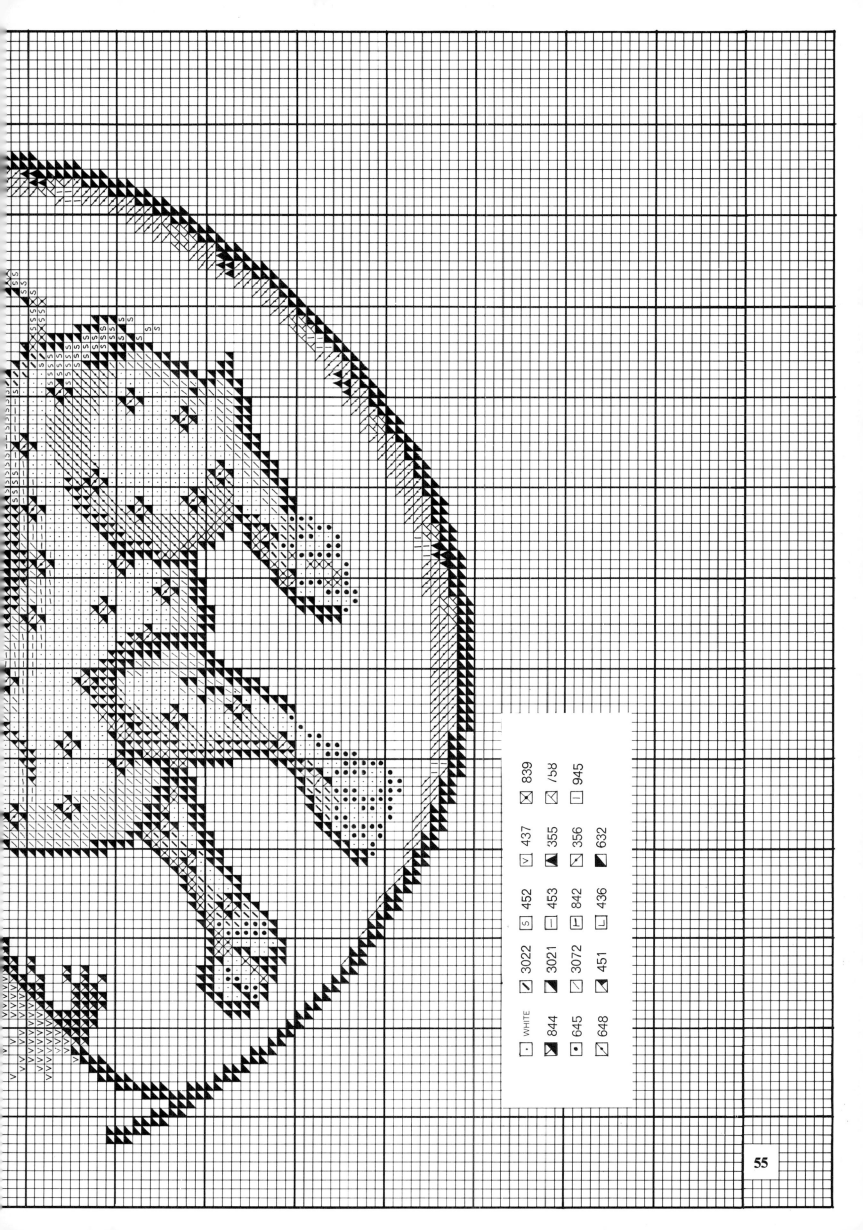

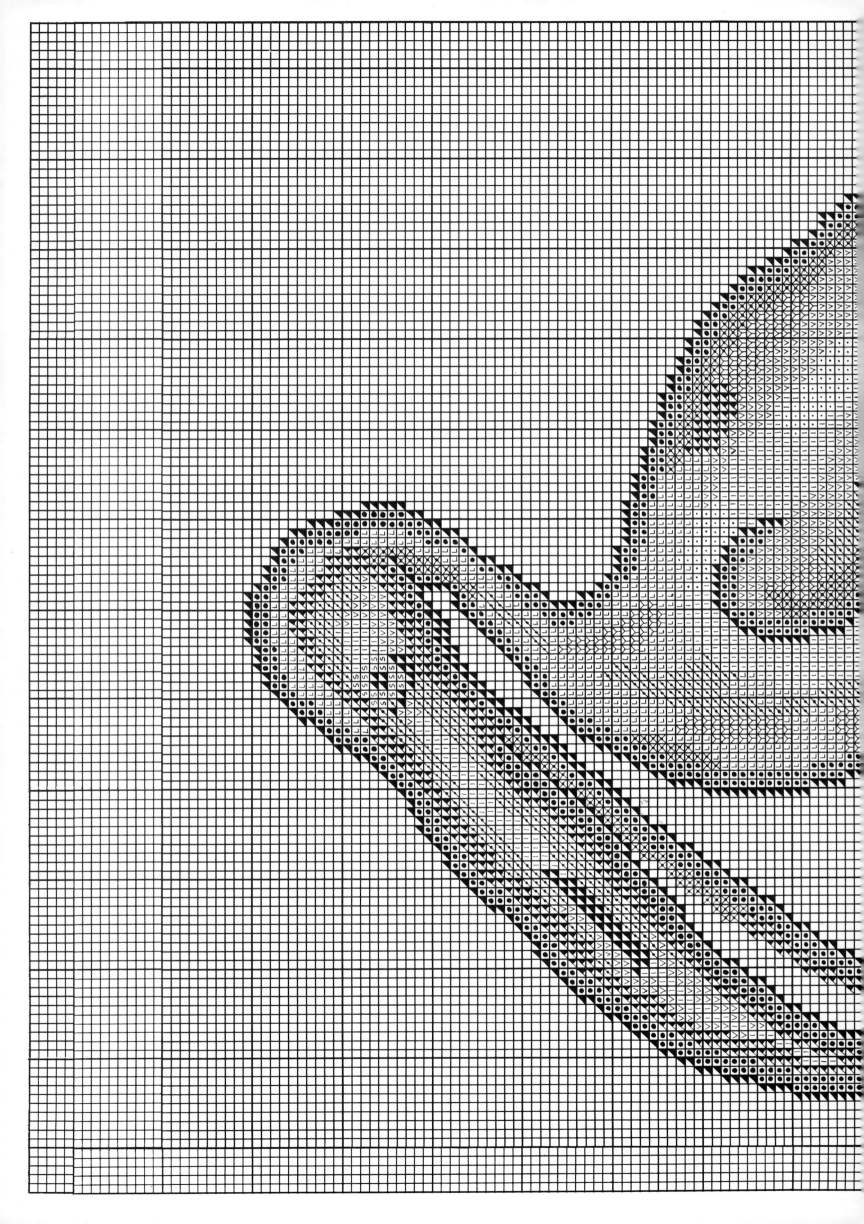

436	823
833	920
3046	677
680	930
729	726
	OFF-WHITE

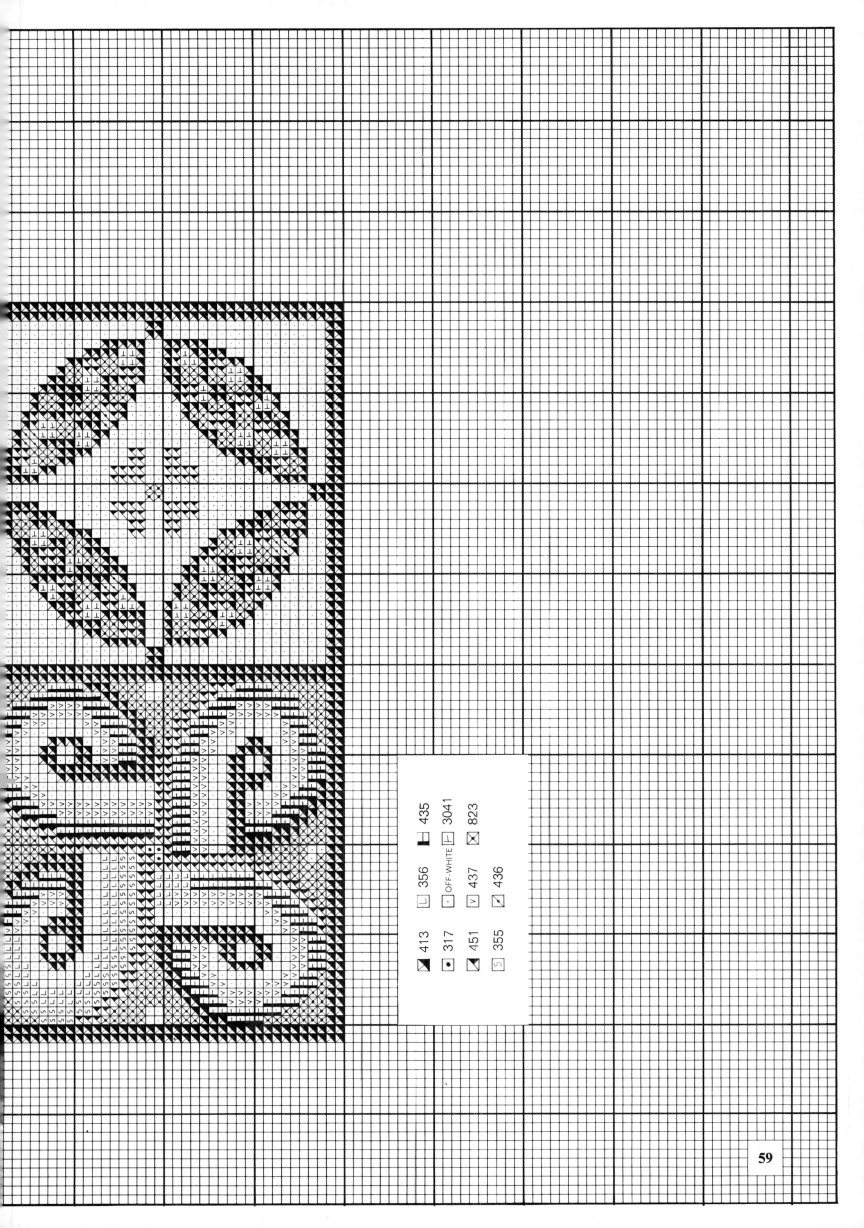

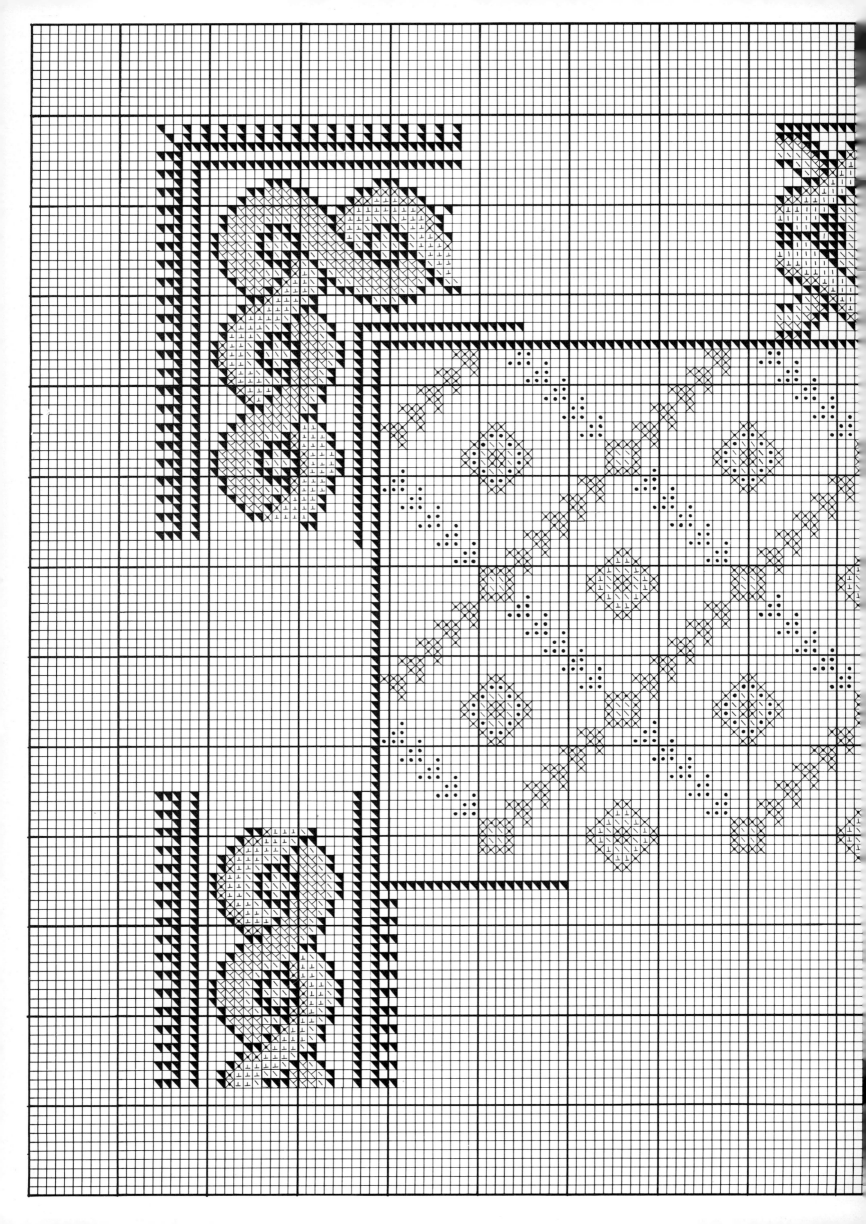

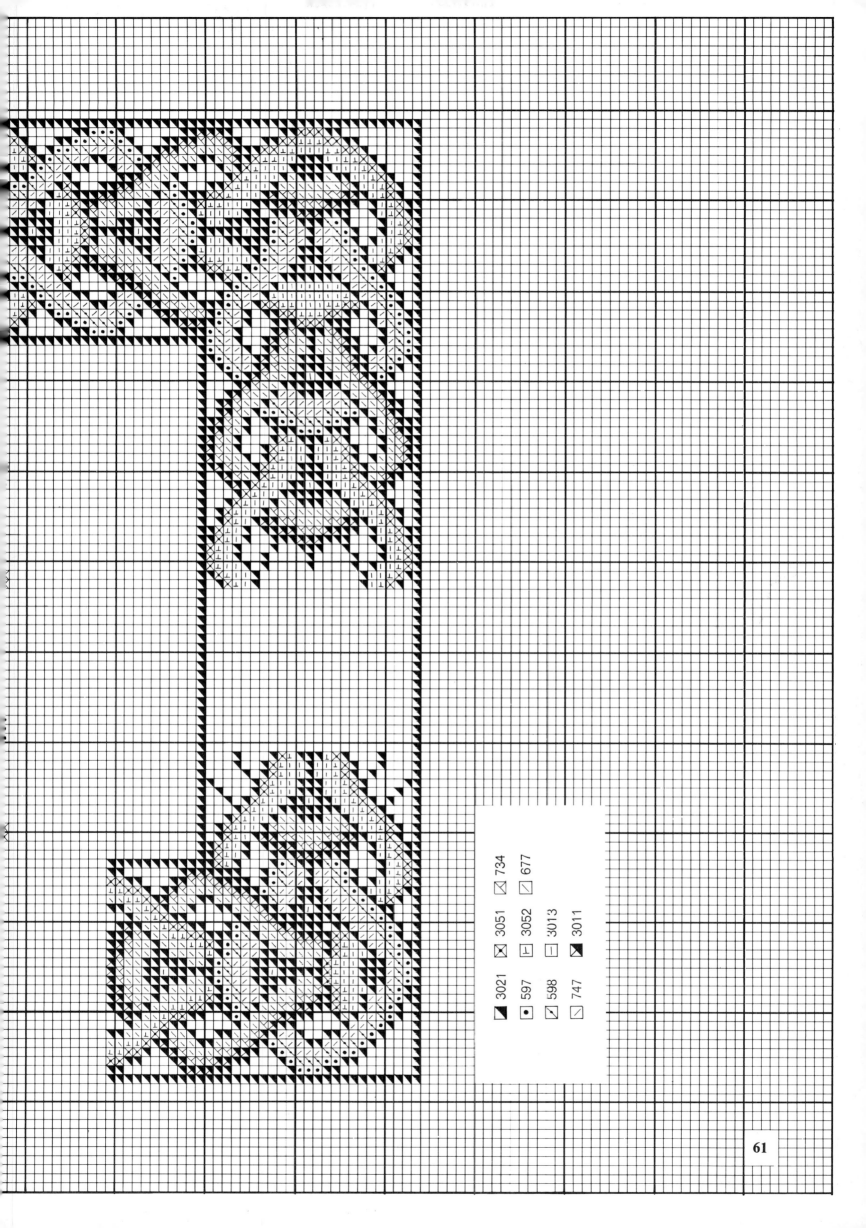

◥ 3021	⊠ 3051	⊠ 734	⧄ 677
• 597	⊤ 3052	▭ 3013	◹ 3011
⟋ 598	⧄ 747		

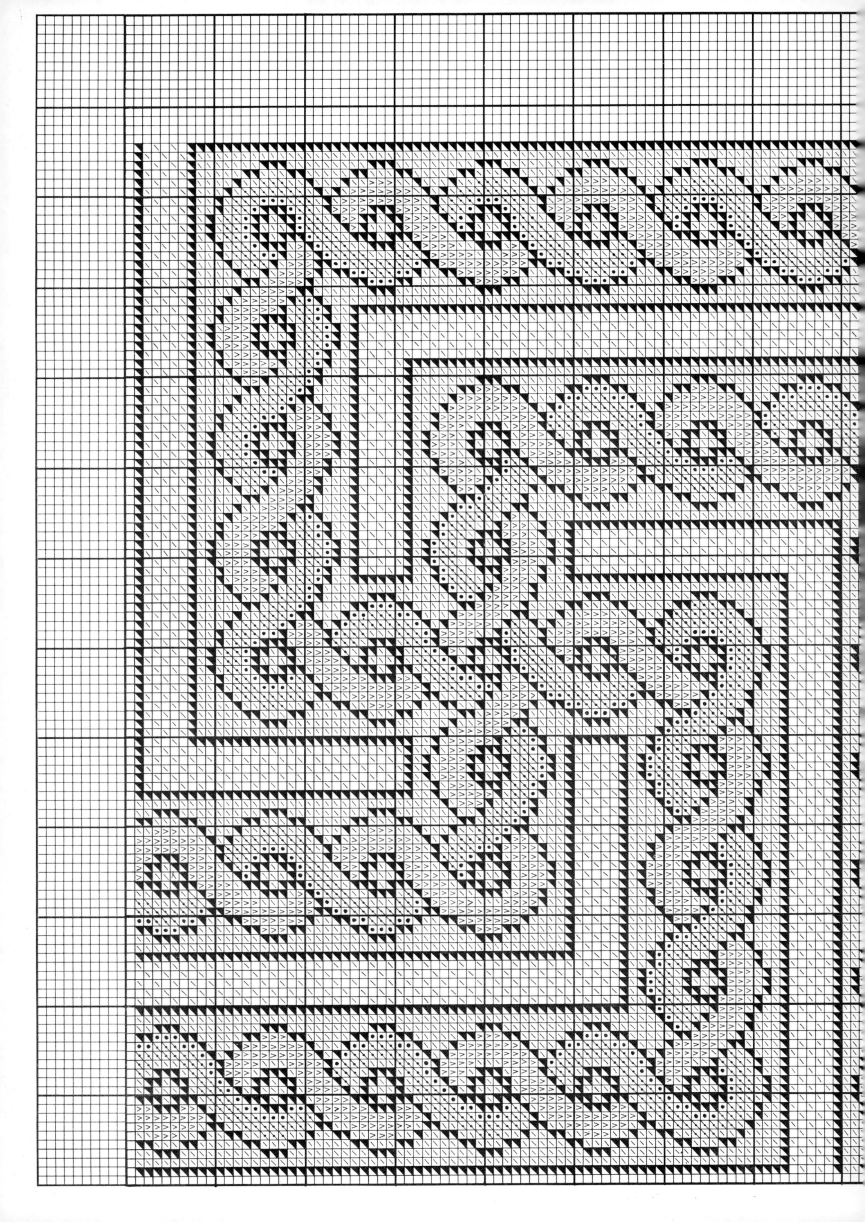

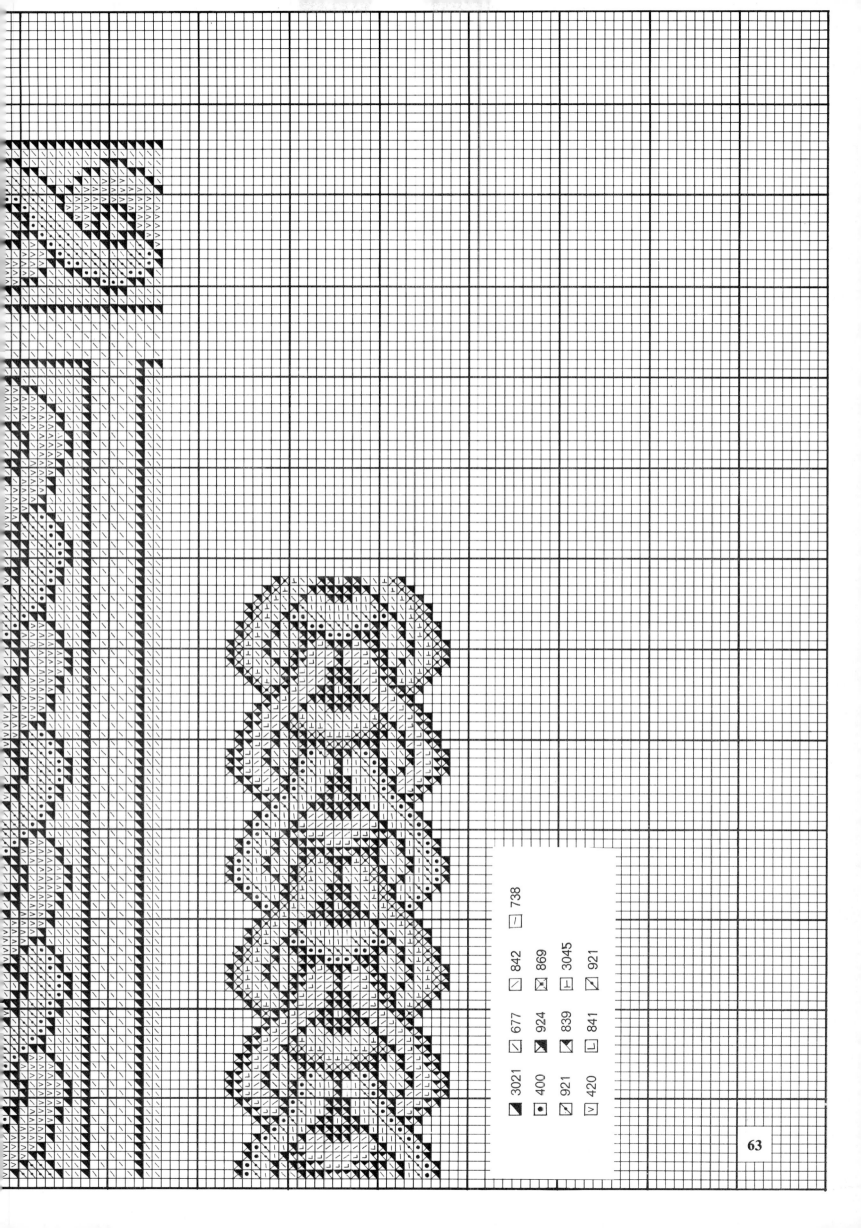

◪ 3021	⬜ 842	⊟ 738
⊡ 400	⬛ 924	
◪ 921	◣ 839	
▽ 420	⬜ 841	
	◪ 677	⊠ 869
		⊟ 3045
		◪ 921